STECK-VAUGHN
PORTRAIT OF AMERICA

Oregon

Steck-Vaughn Company
  Executive Editor   Diane Sharpe
  Senior Editor   Martin S. Saiewitz
  Design Manager   Pamela Heaney
  Photo Editor   Margie Foster
  Electronic Cover Graphics Alan Klemp

Proof Positive/Farrowlyne Associates, Inc.
Program Editorial, Revision Development, Design, and Production

Consultant: Oregon Tourism Commission

Published by Raintree Steck-Vaughn Publishers, an imprint of Steck-Vaughn Company.

A Turner Educational Services, Inc. book. Based on the Portrait of America television series by R. E. (Ted) Turner.

Cover Photo: Crater Lake by © Michael Reagan, TBS, Inc.

Library of Congress Cataloging-in-Publication Data

Thompson, Kathleen.
    Oregon / Kathleen Thompson.
      p. cm. — (Portrait of America)
    "Based on the Portrait of America television series" — T.p. verso.
    "A Turner book."
    Includes index.
    ISBN 0-8114-7382-1 (library binding). — ISBN 0-8114-7463-1 (softcover)
    1. Oregon—Juvenile literature. [1. Oregon.] I. Title.
    II. Series: Thompson, Kathleen. Portrait of America.
    F876.3.T46 1996
    979.5—dc20   95-50399
                                                     CIP
                                                      AC

Printed and Bound in the United States of America

1 2 3 4 5 6 7 8 9 10 WZ 98 97 96 95

Acknowledgments
The publishers wish to thank the following for permission to reproduce photographs:
P. 7 © Park Street; p. 8 © Brian Stablyk/Tony Stone Images; p. 10 (top) USDA Forest Service, (bottom) Oregon Historical Society; p. 11 (top) Fort Clatsop National Memorial, National Park Service, (bottom) Beinecki Library, Yale University; p. 12 Oregon Historical Society; p. 13 (top) McLouglin Memorial, (bottom) Oregon Historical Society; pp. 15 (both), 16, 17 (both) Oregon Historical Society; p. 18 Portland District, U.S. Army Corps of Engineers; p. 19 (top) © Charlotte A. Becker/Association of Oregon Recyclers, (bottom) © Jack Wilburn/Animals Animals; p. 20 AP/Wide World; p. 21 © Gary Braasch; pp. 22, 23 (both) Oregon Historical Society; p. 24 Nike; p. 26 Boise Cascade, Oregon; p. 27 © Superstock; p. 28 (top) © Superstock, (bottom) Nut Growers Society of Oregon, Washington; p. 29 State of Oregon Travel Information; pp. 30, 31, 32, © Gary Braasch; p. 33 (top) American Forest Institute, (bottom) © Gary Braasch; p. 34 © Superstock; p. 36 (top) State of Oregon Travel Information, (bottom) © Gayle Hoffman; p. 37 (top) Oregon Shakespearean Festival Association, (bottom) USDA Forest Service; p. 38 (top) Sea Lions Caves Inc., (bottom) USDA Forest Service; p. 39 © Superstock; pp. 40, 41 USDA Forest Service; pp. 42, 44 © Superstock; p. 46 One Mile Up; p. 47 (left) One Mile Up, (center) © N. M. Hauprich/Photo Researchers, (right) North Dakota Tourism.

Oregon

Kathleen Thompson

A Turner Book

RSVP

RAINTREE
STECK-VAUGHN
PUBLISHERS
The Steck-Vaughn Company

Austin, Texas

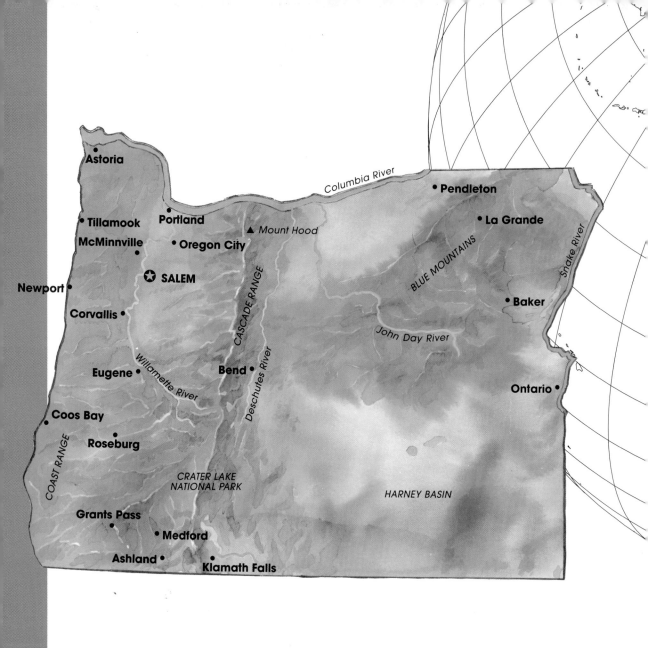

Astoria

Columbia River

Pendleton

Tillamook   Portland
                                    ▲ Mount Hood   La Grande
McMinnville   Oregon City

Newport   ☆ SALEM

Corvallis   Baker

                              John Day River
Eugene   Bend

Coos Bay   Deschutes River

Roseburg   Ontario

COAST RANGE

CASCADE RANGE

BLUE MOUNTAINS

Snake River

Willamette River

CRATER LAKE
NATIONAL PARK   HARNEY BASIN

Grants Pass

Medford

Ashland

Klamath Falls

Oregon

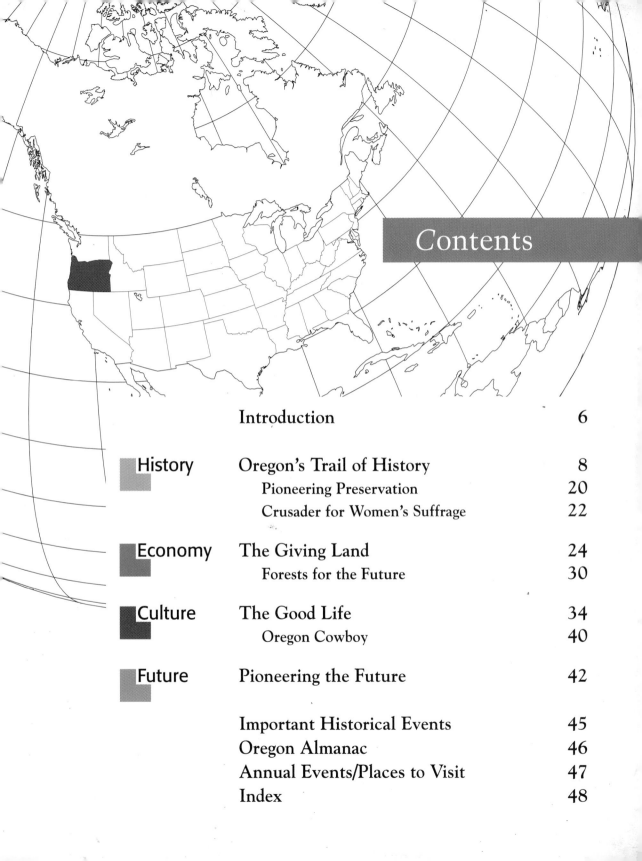

Contents

Introduction

Oregon is called the "Pacific Wonderland." It's a fitting name for a state so beautiful. That name also goes a long way in describing the variety of life forms and landscapes that are found in the state. The Cascade Mountains create a natural barrier in Oregon, dividing the state into two very different sections. The western section features hundreds of miles of exciting coastline. The Willamette Valley is home to many of the state's larger cities and almost half of Oregon's residents. East of the Cascades is a wonderland of variable landscapes, featuring desert plains, lush forest hills, deep canyons, and towering waterfalls. From wheat fields to flower gardens, whale watching to cattle herding, the best of the West is in Oregon.

The Painted Hills at John Day Fossil Beds National Monument, near Mitchell, contain plant and animal fossils that are more than 45 million years old.

Oregon

Oregon's Trail of History

By about 1500 well over one hundred Native American groups lived in present-day Oregon. The largest group was the Chinook. They lived in the northwestern region near the mouth of the Columbia River. The Chinook traded dried fish and other items with inland groups.

To the east of the Chinook lived the Nez Percé. Around 1700 these people became the first group in the area to raise horses. This form of transportation allowed the Nez Percé to extend the territory over which they hunted and traded with other groups. The Nez Percé also were skilled fishers, and they lived largely on salmon from the Columbia River.

In the mountainous southwestern part of the Oregon area lived the Klamath and the Modoc. These people lived mostly on fish, too, from Lake Klamath and smaller area lakes and ponds. They also ate seeds and roots. These groups built winter homes made from earth and wood. In summer they lived in *wickiups*—wood-frame homes covered with grasses and reeds.

The crew of the Lewis and Clark expedition built Fort Clatsop in December 1805. Living-history guides at the reconstructed fort demonstrate pioneer skills, such as cleaning a deer hide.

above. This rich land by the Snake River was occupied by the Nez Percé before they were forced to live on federal reservations.

below. Ancient Native American petroglyphs on canyon walls at the Dalles tell a story of early Oregon history.

. The Paiute lived in the area to the east of the Klamath Mountains. Their food consisted mainly of rabbits, snakes, insects, roots, and berries. Their cone-shaped homes were made from brush, and they were known for their skill as basket weavers.

British explorer James Cook and his party met the Chinook near the mouth of the Columbia River in 1778. The explorer and his crew exchanged weapons, utensils, and clothing for seal, otter, and beaver pelts.

Ten years later, in 1788, Robert Gray reached the shore of present-day Oregon. In 1792 Gray became the first non–Native American to explore the Columbia River. The Columbia wasn't explored further for another 13 years, until Meriwether Lewis and William Clark arrived at its mouth in 1805. The Lewis and Clark expedition had been sent by the federal government to explore the western part of the continent. Once Lewis and Clark reached present-day Oregon, they traded with the Nez Percé, who helped them complete their journey.

The area known as the Oregon Country included all of today's Oregon, Washington, and Idaho, as well as parts of Wyoming, Montana, and Canada. In 1811 John Jacob Astor, an American fur trader, started the first settlement in the Oregon Country. It was a fur-trading post called Astoria, at the mouth of the Columbia River. Astor lost his trading post one year later when the War of 1812 broke out between Great Britain and the United States over land and trade disputes. Astor's fur trade was taken over by the British North West Company.

In 1818 the United States and Great Britain agreed to share the occupation of the Oregon Country

above. During the winter of 1805–1806, Lewis and Clark stayed at Fort Clatsop, near today's Astoria. The fort has been restored and designated a national memorial.

below. This map was used by Lewis and Clark on their journey through Oregon.

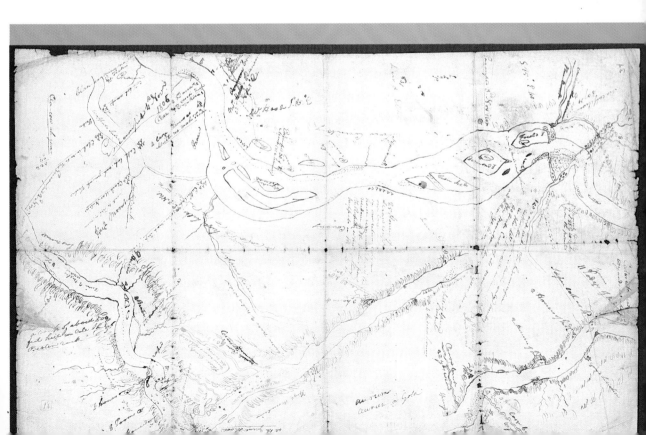

for ten years. By the early 1820s, another British trading firm called the Hudson's Bay Company commanded all fur-trading operations in the Oregon Country. Both the United States and Great Britain renewed their joint-ownership agreement in 1827, this time without setting a time limit.

By the early 1840s, groups of settlers began making the overland journey from Independence, Missouri, across the Great Plains and the Rocky Mountains to the Oregon Country. They followed the Oregon Trail, a route that had been used by trappers and explorers traveling to the West. In 1843 the trail's first wagon train, which included almost one thousand settlers, arrived in Oregon. In two years five thousand settlers were living in the Willamette Valley south of the Columbia River. Thousands more braved the difficult journey over the next forty years.

A national mood of expansionism led to the election of President James K. Polk in 1844. In his first speech as President, Polk claimed the Oregon Country as sole property of the United States. In 1846 Polk terminated the territorial agreement with Great Britain and set the northwest border of the United States at the southern tip of Alaska. Great Britain offered the present-day boundary instead, and Polk and Congress agreed to the British proposal.

The arrival of so many settlers in the Oregon Country caused problems for the Native Americans living in the area. The settlers disrupted the Native Americans' traditional hunting grounds and fishing areas. Gradually the Native Americans were forced to

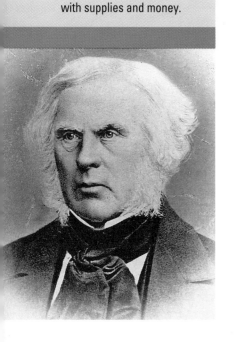

As head of the Hudson's Bay Company, John McLoughlin was told to try to keep American settlers out of the Oregon Country, to save the land for British settlement. McLoughlin is known as the Father of Oregon largely because he ignored these orders and even furnished the American newcomers with supplies and money.

John McLoughlin's home in Oregon City, built in 1845–1846, is now a national historic site.

live on smaller areas of land. The settlers were causing other problems, too. The Native Americans began catching European diseases such as smallpox and cholera. Because Native Americans had no natural immunity to such diseases, sickness spread through their villages very quickly.

The federal government began pressuring Native Americans to sign treaties. These agreements would secure Native Americans their own land, or reservations, if they would promise to remain there. Reservation land often lacked enough good soil and water for Native Americans to sustain themselves, however. In addition, reservation officials often failed to provide the food, education, and money that the government treaties had promised.

Hostilities between the Native Americans and settlers began in 1847. A group of Cayuse attacked a missionary camp in the southern Washington

These wagon ruts were caused by wagon trains that carried settlers and their possessions over the 2,170-mile Oregon Trail.

13

area, killing 15 people. When the Oregon settlers heard of the attack, they began burning Cayuse camps. This action sparked the Cayuse War. News of the Cayuse War and other Native American battles reached Washington, D.C. The federal government realized that Oregon would need to organize and establish a government to protect its settlers. Congress acted quickly and made Oregon an official territory in 1848. The Native American battles were far from over, however.

Two major Native American battles were fought in the Oregon Territory in the 1850s. The Rogue River Indian War began when gold was discovered near Jackson Creek in 1851. The war lasted until 1856, when the area's remaining Native Americans were forced onto a reservation.

The Yakima Indian War began in Washington in 1855 when the Yakima refused to leave their homeland to live on a reservation. The war spread into northern Oregon, and other Native American groups came to the aid of the Yakima. When the war ended in 1858, the Yakima and all other groups who had fought in the war were forced onto the Yakima reservation in southwestern Washington.

In 1859 Oregon was admitted to the Union as the thirty-third state. By 1860 the population of Oregon had more than quadrupled since its beginnings as a territory, reaching well over fifty thousand.

Around 1870 the Modoc, who lived along the southern border of Oregon, were moved to a reservation that was already occupied by the Klamath. Since the Klamath had been there first, most of the supplies and food rationed to the reservation went to them. The Modoc were beginning to starve when their leader Kintpuash, nicknamed Captain Jack, left the reservation to find food. In November 1872 federal troops came after the Modoc to return them to the reservation by force. For almost eight months, the Modoc hid in lava beds on the California and Oregon border. This barren terrain had many cracks and caves to hide in. In May 1873, however, the Modoc were at last forced to surrender. Captain Jack was later hanged.

The final major Native American battle in Oregon was the Nez Percé War. The Nez Percé, too, fought against confinement on the reservations. In May 1877 Nez Percé leader Chief Joseph led a group of about eight hundred of his people on a flight to Canada. After outwitting the pursuing federal troops numerous times, the group was finally surrounded in Montana that September, less than a day away from the Canadian border. Chief Joseph and most of his followers were sent

On his deathbed Chief Joseph's father told him, "This country holds your father's body. Never sell the bones of your father and mother." These words made Joseph especially unwilling to move to a reservation.

A cavalry soldier looks in on a family of settlers traveling to the West in the 1870s.

The opening day of the Northern Pacific Railroad on September 11, 1883, celebrated a link by rail from Portland, Maine, to Portland, Oregon.

to a reservation in Washington. Joseph died on the reservation in 1904. It was said that he died of "a broken heart" for his lost Oregon homeland.

With the major Native American battles at an end, the people of Oregon concentrated on building the state's economy. Mining, farming, ranching, and logging were the state's main economic activities. The development of railroad lines to other western states, beginning in the 1860s, improved trade. When the Northern Pacific Railroad was completed in 1883, Oregon's markets stretched from Portland to cities in the east.

Besides opening economic opportunities, the railroads were also providing opportunities for corruption. Railroad owners began charging farmers extremely high shipping prices. In 1873 a number of farmers established the Oregon State Grange. This organization worked with the state legislature to end the abuses of the railroad companies. In 1892 farmers also helped bring about a reform movement called the People's party. The Populists, as they were called, fought for the rights of farmers, workers, and small business owners. The Populists managed to pass many laws and gain influence in the state government.

Oregon's economy continued to grow until the Great Depression settled upon the entire nation in the 1930s. Banks and other businesses across the nation were forced to close down. Thousands of Oregonians lost their jobs. Farmers and ranchers had to sell their products at very low prices during this period.

To help provide jobs for the nation's unemployed workers, the federal government created projects to build public structures. In 1933 the United States government began construction of the Bonneville Dam on the Columbia River. The job was completed in 1937. In addition to putting people to work, the dam spurred Oregon's industry by providing hydroelectric power to the area.

The United States entered World War II in December 1941, when Japanese forces bombed the United States military base at Pearl Harbor, Hawaii. Oregon's factories and farms began supplying food and military equipment to troops overseas. Portland also became a center for shipbuilding.

The federal government was afraid that people of Japanese descent would spy on America's government and military. In 1942 Congress approved the relocation of thousands of Japanese Americans living in California, Oregon,

above. During World War II, millions of American women worked in defense plants to replace men who joined the military.

below. During World War II, thousands of people moved to Portland to work in its shipyards building warships.

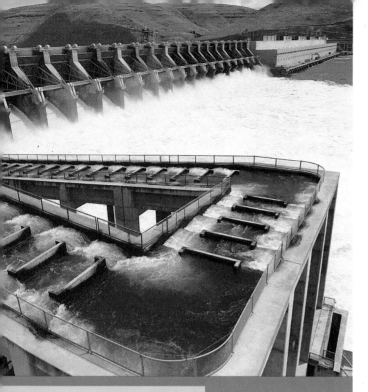

The John Day Dam, on the Columbia River, was built in 1968 to provide flood control, hydroelectric power, and irrigation. This dam contains a fish ladder (foreground), a kind of watery staircase that allows migrating salmon to cross the dam unharmed.

and Washington to internment camps in the interior states. More than one hundred thousand Japanese Americans were relocated between 1942 and the end of the war in 1945. When these innocent people were released, most of them had lost their jobs and their possessions.

After the war, industry grew in Oregon once again. In addition to electricity, the Bonneville Dam and several other new dams provided water for irrigation. Many farms were opened in areas that had previously been too dry to support crops. A new wave of immigrants, mostly from Mexico, came to work on Oregon's quickly expanding farms and factories.

The lumber industry was also booming. During the 1950s and 1960s, the country's population increased greatly. More new homes and larger homes were being built across the country. In the 1960s more than half of the new homes in the nation were built with Oregon lumber.

At the same time, however, there were growing efforts to conserve Oregon's resources, especially its forests. The logging industry began planting trees to replace the ones cut down. Logging companies looked for ways to use every part of the trees, including bark and sawdust. All former waste products were now used for products such as plywood and pulp.

The boost in the logging industry did not last, however. The first half of the 1980s was very difficult as construction across the nation declined, lowering the demand for Oregon's wood products. Other businesses, especially those that depended on a strong lumber industry, began to suffer as well. Oregon's unemployment rates during this period were among the worst in the country.

Oregon's struggling economy recovered in the second half of the 1980s, however. One reason was the growth of electronics manufacturing. These businesses had already been part of Oregon's economy, but new demand for computers and other high-tech machines created a number of new jobs.

Oregon has not allowed its economy to compromise its environment. Local rulings in the 1990s, for the most part, have held businesses responsible for their environmental impact. Some of Oregon's residents are still concerned about the environment. Throughout the 1990s, Oregon has been in the national spotlight because of its endangered resident, the spotted owl. As the logging industry continues its expansion, these owls and their habitat have been slowly disappearing. But Oregon's economy will suffer if the logging industry is only allowed to harvest a limited number of trees. Oregon's struggles to balance its economy with environmental concerns are being followed closely across the nation. Although environmental issues are common in many communities, few other issues will have as important an impact on so many lives.

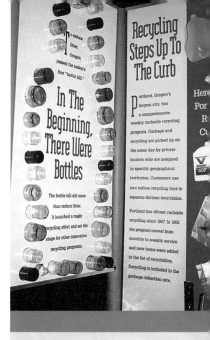

above. In an effort to preserve the environment, Portland residents recycle as many products as possible instead of throwing them away.

below. In 1990 the federal government declared Oregon's spotted owl an endangered species.

Pioneering Preservation

While much of this country has been tamed by roads and railways, Oregon has managed to maintain areas of wilderness. Many people believe, however, that it's just a matter of time before Oregon's wilderness is tamed, too. They believe that you just can't stand in the way of progress. But if that were true, Oregon would have become urbanized long ago. Instead, Oregon has pioneered conservation laws, proving that progress doesn't always have to mean environmental destruction.

Oregon began its environmental pioneering when residents elected former journalist Tom McCall to the governorship in 1966. McCall was known for his concern for Oregon's environment, and much of his journalistic career had centered on exposing the state's growing pollution problems. McCall helped enact laws that gave residents, not corporations, the final say on how their land would be used.

Thanks to these laws, almost eight hundred thousand acres of forest and

After helping to get Oregon's bottle deposit legislation passed, Tom McCall campaigned on behalf of a similar law in California.

hundreds of miles of coastline are protected from logging and construction. Rivers that used to be too dirty to even stick your feet into are now full of swimmers, boaters, and fishers. In the 1970s Oregon also pioneered recycling laws, becoming the first state to require all soft drink cans and bottles to be returnable and recyclable. This cut down on littering in the state, because people would save their bottles and cans for a refund rather than throw them carelessly away in Oregon's parks and rivers.

Oregon also became one of the few states of the nation to discourage new business in the state. Its legislators and its people truly believed that the environment could not endure a larger population. Governor McCall even went so far as to tell a group of potential residents to find somewhere else to settle.

Before his death in the early 1980s, Tom McCall was worried that the environmental progress of Oregon would be reversed as environmentalism began to go out of fashion. It doesn't look like McCall had anything to worry about, however. Oregon has continued to pass legislation to protect its environment. The nationwide—and worldwide—struggle to protect the environment continues to be a tough battle, but Oregon continues to hold its own.

Many of Oregon's farms depend on water provided by the Willamette River.

Crusader for Women's Suffrage

For many people it is hard to imagine a time when women were not allowed to vote in state, local, and national elections. But in most of the United States, women didn't have that right until early in the twentieth century. In the Pacific Northwest, women's suffrage, or right to vote, was an uphill battle. It was a battle won largely through the efforts of Abigail Scott Duniway.

In the 1860s women were not expected to manage household money or to work at any kind of business. Society did not think them capable of doing a good job. In addition, certain laws had been passed limiting the rights of women to own property. Abigail Scott Duniway realized that the only way to ensure equal rights for women was to change the laws. The only way to change the laws was for women to win the right to vote.

In 1871 Duniway established her own newspaper, the *New Northwest*. In it she spoke out against the unfair treatment of women. It was the start of her crusade for women's suffrage. In 1873 she helped found the Oregon State Suffrage Association. Duniway's rapid progress convinced her that she could win the fight for equal rights within five years.

Duniway traveled all over the Pacific Northwest—Oregon, Idaho, and Washington—giving speeches and gathering support. Men as well as women came to listen to Duniway's

Abigail Scott Duniway was one of the original pioneers on the Oregon Trail, which she traveled at age 17.

For 16 years Abigail Scott Duniway published the *New Northwest, a newspaper dedicated to promoting equal rights for women.*

passionate speeches. But not everyone was delighted about the changes Duniway proposed. During a speech in one small town, an angry crowd showered her with eggs. The police had to be called in to help Duniway get safely out of town.

In 1896 the Idaho legislature granted women the right to vote. Duniway was determined to see her own state of Oregon do the same. She campaigned for women's suffrage

harder than ever. In 1900 Duniway managed to get suffrage on the state ballot. It lost—but by a narrow margin. The closeness of the vote encouraged Duniway. She was determined to work even harder.

By 1912 Duniway had become a symbol for women's rights and one of the most respected figures in the state of Oregon. Her crusade for women's suffrage in Oregon had gone on for 41 years! When the suffrage bill was again placed on the ballot, the people of Oregon voted to pass it. It took almost a half century of struggle, but her dream of equal rights for women had finally become a reality.

Abigail Scott Duniway voted for the first time when she was almost eighty years old.

The Giving Land

· Much of Oregon's economy comes from its natural resources. Its trees, soil, and grazing lands have long provided a solid foundation for the state. Oregon's powerful rivers help provide energy for a booming manufacturing industry. Minerals play a significant role in the mining industry. The state's natural resources contribute in another way. The variety and beauty of the landscape help to maintain one of the most successful tourist industries in the nation.

Manufacturing is the most important economic activity in Oregon. About 225,000 people are employed making products, mostly out of resources found within the state. Each year these workers contribute almost $15 billion to Oregon's economy.

The most important area of manufacturing in Oregon is wood processing. In fact, Oregon produces more lumber than any other state. In past years Oregon's lumber industry provided mainly wood for construction. Today Oregon's lumber industry makes

Nike, one of the world's leading wholesale distributors of athletic shoes and sportswear, is based in Beaverton. More Oregonians are employed by wholesale and retail trade than by any other industry.

Oregon's paper mills use millions of tons of lumber from the state's forests each year.

many other products, such as furniture, particle board, plywood, and paper, from its harvested trees.

The second largest area of manufacturing in Oregon is food processing. A number of plants are located in the Willamette Valley. These companies pack, can, freeze, or otherwise prepare fruits and vegetables grown in the valley. A number of meat- and seafood-processing plants are also located in that area. In all, food processing adds well over one billion dollars to the state's economy each year.

Oregon's fastest-growing area of manufacturing is high-technology products such as electronic components and computers. Portland, Salem, and Eugene are the main areas where this industry is concentrated. Computer software companies are also on the rise. In fact, Oregon has established a Software Association to encourage further development of this profitable high-tech industry.

Other areas of manufacturing that are on the rise in Oregon are biotechnology and plastics. In addition, the well-known athletic footwear company Nike, Inc., is headquartered in Beaverton, just outside of Portland. Nike employs over 2,500 of Oregon's manufacturing workers.

Oregon's water resources also play a significant role in the state's economy. Fishers harvest about one hundred million pounds of fish and shellfish each year. Oregon is best known for its salmon harvests, but clams, cod, scallops, and crabs are among the other popular catches in the state.

Minerals are another of Oregon's profitable natural resources. Every county of Oregon has at least one mine or quarry. Sand and gravel are most important to the state, but limestone, gypsum, and pumice are also mined. Metals are less plentiful, but there are a few gold mines, as well as copper, silver, and bauxite mines.

Although Oregon doesn't depend on agriculture as much as it used to, Oregon's farmers are still crucial to the state's economy. Small farms in much of the country have been taken over by large companies. But farming has remained a family business in Oregon. In fact, 99 percent of Oregon's agricultural products are still grown on family-owned farms. The other notable aspect of Oregon's agricultural products is their diversity. Almost 175 different types of crops and agricultural products are produced by Oregon's farmers.

Food processing brings over one billion dollars into Oregon's economy each year.

Oregon's most valuable agricultural products are livestock, especially beef and dairy cattle. About one third of the state's agricultural income comes from livestock. Beef cattle and sheep are raised mostly in the eastern part of the state, while dairy cattle, poultry, and hogs are raised mostly in the west.

Oregon's most valuable crop is wheat, which is grown east of the

Cascade Mountains. Other grain crops include hay, oats, and barley. Some of the main fruits grown in the state are apples, pears, cherries, melons, plums, grapes, and cranberries. Nuts are also an important crop, and Oregon's hazelnut harvests lead the nation. The most important vegetable grown in Oregon is potatoes, followed by corn, sugar beets, onions, peas, and beans.

Greenhouse and nursery products are also crucial to Oregon's agriculture industry. Oregon is one of the nation's leaders in harvesting Christmas trees.

above. This photograph shows a green bean farm in the Willamette Valley.

below. This nut farmer is spraying his trees with pesticides to keep them healthy. Most of Oregon's nut farms are concentrated in the Willamette Valley.

In addition, many farms in the Willamette Valley raise flower bulbs, especially tulips and daffodils.

In recent years Oregon's service industries have grown at a rapid pace. These are jobs in which workers serve other people rather than make products. About three quarters of all the jobs in Oregon are included in this category.

The most important area of service industries in Oregon is wholesale and retail trade. Wholesale trade is the buying and selling of large quantities of goods, usually between businesses. Retail trade is the buying and selling of small quantities of goods, usually to individuals. One example of wholesale trade would be the large quantities of lumber and wheat that Oregon sells to other countries. Retail establishments in Oregon include restaurants, department stores, and car dealerships. In all, over three hundred thousand of Oregon's workers are involved in wholesale and retail trade.

Community, social, and personal services are the second most important category of service industries in Oregon. About 250,000 of Oregon's workers are involved in this type of service work. They include doctors, social workers, clerical workers, and lawyers.

Oregon enjoys a thriving tourist industry due to the efforts of its energetic service workers. Hotel reservation agents, souvenir shop clerks, and rental agents all help make tourism in Oregon a $3.6 billion industry.

Oregon has it all—from plentiful natural resources to thriving cities. These riches, along with its varied economy, hold a promise of prosperity for the new century and beyond.

Millions of tourists visit Oregon every year to experience the view from Hells Canyon and other mountain vistas. Tourists add more than three billion dollars per year to the state economy.

Forests for the Future

Oregon's logging companies are some of the oldest in America. Oregon has long supplied the nation with wood for everything from houses to pencils. Many of Oregon's loggers come from families that have been in the profession since the 1800s. Many of them can't imagine doing anything else for a living.

As one longtime Oregon logger says, "You're out there in the elements, and some days the sun shines and sometimes it's raining, and then it's snowing and blowing and next day it's really hot. So, you just have to love the outdoors or you don't want to be a logger."

Many loggers believe that logging is putting the landscape to good use, like cultivating a garden. As another lifetime logger puts it, "We till the soil, we work it up. We plant our garden in the spring, and it comes up and it gets green and it matures. And so when it matures, we don't just look at it and admire it. We go out and pick the

A logging truck carries logs out of a forest near Tillamook.

tomatoes, we use it. Just like a garden. It just takes a little longer."

Unfortunately, however, it takes a lot longer for trees to grow back than for tomatoes to grow. Tomatoes come up every year, but many of the trees cut from Oregon's forest have taken a century or two to grow. It will take that long for another tree to grow and replace it. Thankfully, there are people trying to replace Oregon's forests, however gradually. One of these groups is called the Hoedads.

The Hoedads were started in 1970. They got their name from the tool, called a hoedag, they used to dig holes for seedling trees. The Hoedads travel to an area that a logging company has clear-cut, or cleared entirely of trees. They camp out for however long it takes to reforest the area, which ranges from hundreds to thousands of acres. It's backbreaking work—each planter has to carry a forty-pound bag of seedlings and hunch over digging holes for long periods.

"You have to have endurance," said a veteran Hoedad. "It gets hot out here. It's dusty, or it's really rainy and miserable. There's a certain persever-ance, a certain roughness you have to

Hoedads plant five hundred to one thou-sand seedlings each day.

have." But every Hoedad agrees, no matter how demanding their work, it's well worth the effort.

As one Hoedad says, "You plant a tree by every stump, so you do feel like you're putting the woods back. And when you go back to a stand where you planted two [to] . . . five years ago, then you feel like, yeah, it is coming back."

Apparently, the Hoedads began their work not a second too late.

31

Wood processing is Oregon's most important manufacturing operation, so it is important for loggers and environmentalists to reach a compromise.

The other problem with clear-cutting is that it destroys an entire animal habitat. An animal that lives in a tree may not be immediately killed when that tree is cut down. But if all the trees in an area are cut down, the animal will have no place to make a new home. In addition, the animal's source of food—maybe mice or a certain type of insect—may have been wiped out during the clear-cutting, leaving the animal to starve.

Many species of animals have approached extinction because of such logging practices. The most recent to come to the attention of environmentalists is the spotted owl. These owls are becoming extinct because they can survive only in the forests made of older trees. Less dense forests grown

Environmentalists began to discover that logging companies were doing more than just creating hillsides full of stumps. Destroying an entire area of forest creates many problems. For one thing, it kills off fungi that help trees grow. This means that even if trees are replanted, they may not be able to thrive without the help of the fungi.

from recent replantation let in too much light for the owl, disrupting its habitat. Oregon has pushed for federal laws to save the spotted owl from extinction by preserving the state's older forests.

When these laws were first passed in 1991, many loggers were angry. They claimed that the economy would be damaged if the state prevented them from logging in the forests of the spotted owl. But in 1994 Oregon's economy was better than ever, with one of the lowest unemployment rates in the nation.

As a longtime Hoedad said, "It's not like the loggers are the bad guys and the tree planters are the good guys." Oregon is proving that a state can protect its environment and its economy at the same time—without taking sides. As environmental issues come to the forefront across the nation and the world, Oregon is an example that all would do well to follow.

Since clear-cutting has proved so destructive to Oregon's environment, many loggers are agreeing to stop the practice, cutting down only some of a forest's trees rather than all of them.

Loggers clear-cut areas that range in size from a few acres to six hundred acres or more.

The Good Life

Life in Oregon is good. For hundreds of years, Oregon's natural resources—particularly its sea life and its fertile soil—have supported Oregon's earliest inhabitants comfortably. Native Americans did not have to struggle with nature to feed themselves. Instead, they devoted much of their time toward various cultural activities.

The Warm Springs Indian Reservation in central Oregon offers visitors a chance to learn about many different Native American cultures. The Museum at Warm Springs houses a collection of art and multimedia exhibits. Visitors can also learn about Native American art at the Oregon Historical Society and the Favell Museum in Klamath Falls.

These museums display many Native American artifacts, such as baskets and totem poles. Some of the most distinctive baskets are made of tree bark. Totem poles are wooden poles that Native Americans carved and painted with bright colors. They served many different purposes. The poles often depicted the figure

This sculpture, "Portlandia," by R. Kaskey, stands outside the Portland Building. In Portland 1.33 percent of the construction cost to build a public building must be used to produce public art.

above. The Pendleton Round-Up, one of the most famous rodeos in the nation, isn't all bronco riding and calf roping. Many members of the nearby Umatilla Indian Reservation also participate in the festivities, with traditional dancing events.

below. These children are participating in Portland's annual Pacific Power Junior Parade.

of a bird or animal that represented the group clan. Some poles were used as grave markers or house posts. Welcoming poles were often placed at the entrance of harbors. Ridicule poles had likenesses that were carved upside down to make fun of someone.

One of the largest Native American groups living along the Northwest Coast is the Chinook. These people were well known for their celebratory feasts, called *potlatches*. This feast, which could last several days, was held after a totem pole was raised or if a local chief paid a visit. During a potlatch the host would bestow many gifts on his guests.

Most people in Oregon today also live near the coast, mostly around the larger cities of Portland, Eugene, and Salem. Like the early Native Americans, Oregonians today like to celebrate nature, especially the various flowers and plants that grow in the lush Willamette Valley. Like the potlatch, the Portland Rose Festival is a party that lasts several days. In Lebanon, south of Salem, people celebrate the ripening of strawberries by baking the "world's largest strawberry shortcake" for their Strawberry Festival. Portland also has many beautiful gardens, and flowers bloom there year-round.

The performing arts are also cause for festivities in Oregon. For example, Ashland hosts the Oregon Shakespeare Festival every year from February through October, and Eugene is home to the Bach Summer Music Festival.

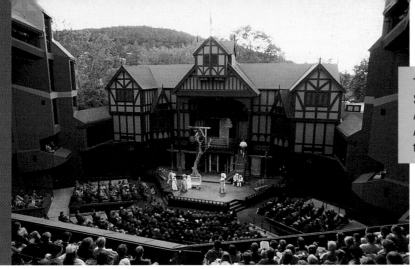

Oregonians' respect for natural things also extends to creatures that make the water their home. Although not a celebration as such, the state was proud to announce two unique aquariums. The Oregon Coast Aquarium in Newport, opened in 1992, is called a natural habitat museum. This means that people can observe ocean animals almost as they are in the wild. The exhibits include caves and underwater canyons. One of the caves is the home of a giant octopus!

The Oregon Rivers Museum is scheduled to open in 1997 in Eugene. The museum will offer a similar natural habitat experience, but for river wildlife rather than ocean wildlife. It will combine elements of both a museum and an aquarium.

Literature has long been a part of the culture in Oregon. The state established its first subscription library in 1834. The Multnomah County Library in Portland opened in 1864 and became the first library in the country to open its doors to the general public. Portland is also home to the largest bookstore in the country, Powell's City of Books.

Multnomah Falls near Portland, another major attraction in Oregon, is one of the highest waterfalls in the nation. Its water drops over six hundred feet.

Oregon has some unique natural attractions, such as the Sea Lion Caves in Florence. Visitors have to travel down two thousand feet in an elevator to get to the caves!

Since the early days of Oregon, lighthouses have kept countless ships from crashing onto the rocky areas of Oregon's shoreline. Shown here is the Heceta Head Lighthouse in Florence.

With such good resources for literature, it's not surprising the number of prominent literary figures who hail from Oregon. Frederic Homer Balch, born in 1861, wrote *The Bridge of the Gods*, about a natural bridge that once crossed the Columbia River. The book is based on a Native American legend about the bridge. Harold Lenoir Davis won the Pulitzer Prize in 1936 for *Honey in the Horn*. Davis specialized in writing stories about the frontier in the west and northwest United States. Ernest Haycox wrote many western novels and screenplays in the mid-1900s, including *Union Pacific*, *Apache Trail*, and *Stagecoach*.

Oregon has also had its share of more modern authors. Ken Kesey, who grew up in Springfield, wrote one of the most famous books of the 1960s, *One Flew Over the Cuckoo's Nest*. The book was later made into a movie. Kesey's novel, *Sometimes a Great Notion*, about a logging family in Oregon, was also made into a movie.

Many of Oregon's modern authors write books for children, too. Beverly Cleary was born in McMinnville in 1916. She has written some of the most popular children's books of all time about three children called Henry Huggins and Beezus and Ramona Quimby. Ursula K. Le Guin has made Portland her home for many years. Le Guin has won many prizes for her children's books and science fiction novels, which include *The Farthest Shore* and *The Left Hand of Darkness*.

Oregon has also raised its share of poets. Edwin Markham, born in 1852 in Oregon City, used his poetry to champion the cause of the working class. Two of his best-remembered poems are "The Man With the Hoe" and "Lincoln, the Man of the People." Poet Phyllis McGinley was born in Ontario, Oregon, in 1905. McGinley was known for her humorous, simple style of writing. This style is often called "light verse." McGinley won a Pulitzer Prize in 1961 for her volume of poetry, *Times Three: Selected Verse from Three Decades*.

Oregon is known around the country as being one of the nicest places to live. The scenery is spectacular, natural resources are abundant, and there are plenty of chances to stop and smell the roses. No wonder people in Oregon believe the good life is all around them!

Hiking is one of the main recreational activities for Oregon's visitors and residents alike.

Oregon Cowboy

John Lane has been an Oregon cowboy all his life. His family has owned his ranch in eastern Oregon since 1918. "Well, my father came from County Kerry [in Ireland]," says Lane. "Came to New York about 1912. Worked in a grocery store as a box boy until he [saved enough money] to come west. And when he came west, he got a job herding sheep. And from there he saved a little money and bought his first ranch in 1918, which we still own."

Becoming a cowboy was a dream fulfilled for John Lane's father. Lane wants to carry on that dream—but it isn't easy. The life of a cowboy means rising with the sun and working ten-hour days. There's branding to be done, fences to build, and hay for winter feeding to gather. Lane also runs a small farm on his land—an especially difficult job with the dry summers and cold winters of eastern Oregon.

John Lane is one of the few ranchers in Oregon who still owns his own land. Many have had to give up ranching because of diminishing profits. In addition, the federal government sometimes reclaims grazing land to protect endangered species. Lane doesn't think this is fair. He doesn't think that the environmentalists who advise the government understand how important these lands are to Oregon cowboys.

"We make a living out of [ranching]," says Lane. "It's our livelihood. . . . Then you have these environmentalists come out, and they say we don't belong here. Well, we've been here all our lives. So it's kind of a hard pill to

In parts of east Oregon, the life of a rancher is much the way it was in the early twentieth century.

swallow when somebody back there'll tell you, 'Well, that's our land,' when all the relatives all the way back down fought for that land and held onto it."

Lane believes that he can take care of his ranching lands just as well as the government could—if not better. "You spend a lifetime developing up an area," he says. "You're not going to quit and walk off. You build it up for everything: for your wildlife, for your cattle, for everybody that's there."

These days there are very few real cowboys left in the nation. Many ranchers use jeeps or helicopters to herd their livestock. Cowboys like John Lane, however, prefer to keep their operations smaller, so that they can get to know their land. But Lane realizes that there aren't many people like him left. "Unless something changes," says Lane sadly, "this way of living that we now know will end." Hopefully Oregon and the government will be able to resolve these land disputes in a way that will preserve both the endangered animal species of Oregon's grasslands—and the endangered species of the American cowboy.

This cattle rancher makes his living in the grassy mountains and valleys of Hells Canyon, in the far eastern part of the state.

41

Pioneering the Future

Oregon's pioneer days ended long ago. Oregon's residents, however, have maintained many of the pioneering attitudes of their ancestors as they plan for the future. These attitudes include healthy amounts of common sense planning, positive attitude, and care for humanity. Oregon's new health care legislation is an example of such pioneering attitude.

In the early 1990s, Oregon took a close look at its state health care coverage. They found that while many higher-income people were getting excellent care, many lower-income people weren't getting any care at all. To solve this problem, Oregon became the first state in the nation to limit the range of services covered, so that more people could receive them. About 120,000 people who had been without health insurance became covered under the new plan.

Oregon's pioneer attitudes toward education have also helped its residents prepare for the future. For example, metropolitan areas are developing communications networks to link the state's schools and

Oregon's youth carry with them the idealism, energy, and positive attitude that has characterized the state for more than two centuries.

As this view of Portland and Mount St. Helens illustrates, the future of Oregon is bound to its landscape and environment.

colleges with research organizations. This helps students gain both education and job preparation.

Sometimes, however, a pioneering spirit can produce mixed results. In the past this has certainly been true in terms of Oregon's land. While dams, irrigation, mining, and logging were often good for Oregon's economy, they sometimes hurt the state's delicate environment. Since the 1960s Oregon has pioneered legislation to protect its resources and environment. But some newer residents think that Oregon's environmental legislation is too strict and would like to see some of the protections on the land lifted.

For some residents the natural beauty of Oregon seems a rare and wonderful thing that should not be touched. But for many others, the land is also a source of income. They feel the land is there to serve their needs. It's a difficult problem. But logical solutions are likely to arise from that Oregonian quality known as the pioneering spirit.

Important Historical Events

1778 British explorer James Cook reaches the mouth of the Columbia River.

1788 Robert Gray becomes the first American to reach Oregon.

1792 Robert Gray discovers the Columbia River and names it after his ship.

1805 Meriwether Lewis and William Clark complete the first known overland journey to the mouth of the Columbia River.

1811 John Jacob Astor establishes Astoria, near the mouth of the Columbia River.

1812 The War of 1812 begins. The British North West Company takes over the Pacific Fur Company.

1825 The British Hudson's Bay Company controls all Oregon Country trading operations.

1834 Oregon establishes its first subscription library.

1843 The first wagon train to travel the Oregon Trail arrives in the Oregon Country with about one thousand settlers.

1846 The Oregon Country is divided at its current boundary between Washington and Canada.

1847 The Cayuse War begins.

1848 The Oregon Territory is created.

1851 Gold is discovered near Jackson Creek, sparking the five-year Rogue River Indian War.

1853 The Washington Territory is created, establishing the boundaries of present-day Oregon.

1855 The three-year Yakima Indian War begins in Washington and spreads to Oregon.

1859 Oregon becomes the thirty-third state.

1872 The Modoc War begins in November and lasts until May 1873.

1873 Farmers' groups form the Oregon State Grange.

1877 Chief Joseph leads a group of Nez Percé on a flight to Canada.

1883 The Northern Pacific Railroad reaches Portland.

1892 The People's party is established in Oregon.

1912 Oregon gives women the right to vote.

1930 The Great Depression sends Oregon and the rest of the nation into economic chaos.

1937 The Bonneville Dam on the Columbia River is completed.

1942 Oregonians of Japanese descent are removed to relocation camps until the end of World War II.

1965 The state's first conservation laws are put into effect.

1971 The Forest Practices Act is passed to conserve Oregon's water, woods, and wildlife. Oregon also passes the nation's first law requiring bottles and cans to be returnable.

1993 The federal government passes legislation limiting logging in older forests to protect the habitat of the spotted owl. Oregon passes its health care plan, which limits services to provide coverage to more people.

45

Oregon's state flag is navy blue and two-sided. A beaver is printed in gold on one side. The other side shows the state seal printed in gold, surrounded by 33 stars, which represent Oregon's entry into the Union as the thirty-third state. The seal shows ships, a pioneer wagon, Douglas firs, a mining pick, a plow, and a sheaf of grain in front of a rising sun.

Oregon Almanac

Nickname. The Beaver State

Capital. Salem

State Bird. Western meadowlark

State Flower. Oregon grape

State Tree. Douglas fir

State Motto. *Alis Volat Propriis* (She Flies with Her Own Wings.)

State Song. "Oregon, My Oregon"

State Abbreviations. Ore. or Oreg. (traditional); OR (postal)

Statehood. February 14th, 1859, the 33rd state

Government. Congress: U.S. senators, 2; U.S. representatives, 5. State Legislature (Legislative Assembly): senators, 30; representatives, 60. Counties: 36

Area. 97,052 sq mi (251,365 sq km), 10th in size among the states

Greatest Distances. north/south, 294 mi (473 km); east/west, 401 mi (645 km). Coastline: 296 mi (476 km)

Elevation. Highest: Mount Hood, 11,239 ft (3,426 m). Lowest: sea level, along the Pacific Ocean

Population. 1990 Census: 2,853,733 (8% increase over 1980), 29th among the states. Density: 29 persons per sq mi (11 persons per sq km). Distribution: 70% urban, 30% rural. 1980 Census: 2,633,149

Economy. *Agriculture:* beef and dairy cattle, sheep, wheat, greenhouse and nursery products, potatoes, apples, pears, cherries, hazelnuts, forest products. *Fishing:* salmon, clams, cod, scallops, crabs. *Manufacturing:* wood processing, food processing, electronic components, computers, software. *Mining:* sand and gravel, limestone, gypsum, pumice, gold, copper, silver, bauxite

State Seal

State Flower: Oregon grape

State Bird:
Western meadowlark

Annual Events

★ Tygh Valley All-Indian Rodeo, at the Dalles (May)

★ Rose Festival and Grand Floral Parade in Portland (June)

★ Sand Castle Contest at Cannon Beach (June)

★ Strawberry Festival in Lebanon (June)

★ International Pinot Noir Celebration in McMinnville (July)

★ World Championship Timber Carnival in Albany (July)

★ Oregon Trail Pageant in Oregon City (July/August)

★ State Fair in Salem (August/September)

★ Round-up and Happy Canyon Pageant in Pendleton (September)

★ Kite Festival in Lincoln City (October)

★ Festival of Lights in Portland (December)

Places to Visit

★ Bonneville Dam, near Cascade Locks

★ Columbia River Gorge and Mount Hood

★ Crater Lake National Park

★ Gilbert House Children's Museum in Salem

★ Hells Canyon National Recreation Area, near La Grande

★ Indian Reservation at Warm Springs

★ Oregon Caves National Monument in southwestern Oregon

★ Oregon Coast Aquarium in Newport

★ Oregon Historical Society in Portland

★ Pacific Northwest Museum of Natural History in Ashland

★ Round-Up Hall of Fame in Pendleton

Index